SELECTED POEMS OF

Gabriela Mistral

INDIANA UNIVERSITY POETRY SERIES

Editor: SAMUEL YELLEN

SELECTED POEMS OF

Gabriela Mistral

Godoy Alcayaga, Lucila

translated by Langston Hughes

INDIANA UNIVERSITY PRESS

BLOOMINGTON

Contents

6

Introduction

She did not sign her poetry with her own name, Lucila Godoy y Alcayaga, because as a young teacher she feared, if it became known that she wrote such emotionally outspoken verses, she might lose her job. Instead she created for herself another name— taking from the archangel Gabriel her first name, and from a sea wind the second. When the poems that were quickly to make her famous, *Sonetos de la Muerte*, were published in 1914, they were signed Gabriela Mistral.

She was born in 1889 in the Chilean village of Vicuña on the River Elqui in a valley where the sweetest of grapes grow. She grew up in the little town of Montegrande where her father was a schoolmaster, and she in turn became a teacher in rural schools, sometimes walking miles into the country to meet her classes. Her father made up verses for village fiestas and, as a young woman, his daughter composed little poems for texts to help children learn to read. She met a young man, Romelio Ureta, with whom she fell in love, but they were never married. For reasons unrelated to their friendship, Ureta committed suicide. Out of love for him and of her desolation at his death came the first of a series of poems soon to be read throughout all Latin America. These included *Sonnets of Death, Prayer,* and the *Poem of the Son,* in whose stark beauty and intensity her personal tragedy "lost its private character and became a part of world literature. It was then that Lucila Godoy y Alcayaga became Gabriela Mistral."

As her renown as a poet grew, so grew her reputation as a teacher of children. The young woman who had no children of her own took her work as an educator very seriously, and explored what was for Chile and the times the most progressive methods of enlightening young minds—visual aids, extracts from great literature, games sometimes in place of books. At first in country schools and coastal villages, then in Santiago de Chile she became an influence in educational circles, and soon was given a government post in the Department of Education at the capital. A group of teachers brought about the publication of her first book—happily for us, in the United States. Federico de Onis, Professor of Spanish Literature at Columbia University in New York, one day gave a talk about her and a reading of a few of her poems. This so inspired his students—most of whom were (or intended to be) teachers of Spanish—that they wanted to lay hands on more of her work. Then they learned that as yet no volume of her poems had been printed. Gabriela Mistral's first book, *Desolacion*, was published by the Spanish Institute of Columbia University in 1922. It has since been reprinted in various editions in South America, each time containing more poems as well as revised versions of previous work, for Gabriela Mistral rewrote often.

In Madrid in 1924 *Ternura* was published. In Buenos Aires in 1938 appeared a third small volume, *Tala*, the proceeds of whose sale went to the relief of the Basque orphans of the Spanish Civil War. In 1954 *Lagar* appeared in Chile, and there that same year a new edition of *Desolacion* was printed. In 1950 in Santiago the *Poemas de las Madres* (included in *Desolacion*) had appeared separately in a beautiful limited edition with drawings by Andre Racz. By then in Spanish speaking countries Gabriela's name (and almost everyone in referring to the poet said simply *Gabriela*) had long been a household word. She had become one of the most popular poets of her tongue. Although her first publication was achieved in our country, in Continental Europe her poems were more widely translated than in England or the United States. Even after she was awarded the Nobel Prize for Literature, why so little of Gabriela was translated into English, I do not know. Much of her poetry is simple and direct in language, never high-flown or flowery, and much easier, I think, to translate than most poets writing in Spanish. Since her poetry is so intensely feminine, however, I hesitated to attempt translations myself, hoping that a woman would do so. None did, in terms of a book. So when Bernard Perry of the Indiana University Press requested that I

10

do so, it intrigued me to try—for the simple reason that I liked the poems.

For the most part I have selected from the various books those poems relating to children, motherhood, and love, including the famous *Poem of the Son* and *Prayer* written during her period of complete desolation, after the man for whom she cared so greatly had died by his own hand.

I have no theories of translation. I simply try to transfer into English as much as I can of the literal content, emotion, and style of each poem. When I feel I can transfer only literal content, I do not attempt a translation. For that reason I have not translated the three *Sonetos de la Muerte*. They are very beautiful, but very difficult in their rhymed simplicity to put into an equivalent English form. To give their meaning without their word music would be to lose their meaning.

The music of Gabriela's poetry started around the world a decade or more before she left her native Chile in the early thirties to begin her own travels, first to Mexico, which had asked her assistance in the organization of rural schools and libraries, then to become Chile's delegate to the League of Nations Institute of Intellectual Cooperation. And in 1931 Gabriela Mistral came to the United States as an instructor in Spanish history and civilization at Middlebury and Barnard colleges. Later she represented her government in various diplomatic posts in South America and Europe, and was a member of the United Nations Subcommittee on the Status of Women. For two years, at President Aleman's invitation, she lived in Mexico as a "guest of the nation." She was Chilean Consul in Brazil, Portugal, at Nice, and Los Angeles. Then after a year as Consul at Naples, in 1953 Gabriela Mistral came again to the United States and settled down in a charming house in Roslyn Harbor, Long Island, where she lived until her death. For twenty years before her death, Gabriela had been honored as Chile's only "life consul"—so appointed by a special enactment of the Chilean Congress—her consulate designated to be "wherever she finds a suitable climate for her health and a pleasant atmosphere to pursue her studies." In the end she chose Roslyn Harbor.

Early in the new year of 1957 Gabriela Mistral died. When the news reached Chile, President Ibañez decreed three days of national mourning. In the United Nations she was eulogized. And the press of the world paid her tribute. In an article at the center of a full page devoted to her memory in *The New York Times Book Review*, Mildred Adams wrote, "Gabriela's clarity and precision, her passion and that characteristic which can only be called her nobility of soul are accepted as ideals. She will not quickly vanish from the literary consciousness of those who value the Spanish tongue." And in *El Diario de Nueva York* Ramon Sender said, "There are poets who hide behind their verses. Others give themselves from their first poem, and so it was with Gabriela Mistral."

LANGSTON HUGHES

Citation

The tears of a mother once caused an entire language disdained by polite society to retrieve its nobility and come into its glory through the power of poetry. It is said that the first of two poets to bear the name of the wind of the Mediterranean, Mistral, while still a student, by having written his first verses in French, caused his mother to weep a flood of tears. She was an untutored peasant of Languedoc who did not understand such purity of language. It was then that her son decided to write henceforth in Provençal, his mother tongue. He wrote *Mireio* which recounts the love of a pretty little peasant woman for a poor artisan, a poem from which the perfume of the earth in flower rises. . . . In this way the old language of the troubadours became again the language of poetry. The Nobel Prize for Literature in 1904 brought this event to the attention of the entire world. Ten years later the poet of *Mireio* died.

The same year that World War II began, at the other end of the world among the flowers of Santiago de Chile, a new Mistral came to attention and was awarded the same Prize for her poems of love dedicated to death.

The story of Gabriela Mistral is so well known among the peoples of South America that in going from country to country she has become almost a legend. And now, from the crests of the Cordilleras of the Andes and across the vastnesses of the Atlantic, she has at last come to us that we might recognize her anew in this room, and here she is.

In a little village in the Valley of the Elqui River a few decades ago, a young school teacher was born who was called Lucila Godoy y Alcayaga. Godoy was her father's name, Alcayaga that of her mother, one or the other being of Basque origin. Her father, who was a teacher, improvised verses with facility. This talent in him seemed to be related to that restlessness and instability ascribed to poets. He deserted his family while his daughter, for whom he had made a little garden, was still an infant. Her pretty mother, who was to live a long time, has reported that she often came across her small daughter deep in conversation with the birds and flowers of the garden. According to one version of the story, she was dismissed from school. She was evidently considered not gifted enough to have hours of instruction wasted upon her. She learned through self-instruction, and eventually she became a teacher in the little village of Cantera. It was there, at the age of twenty, that her destiny was fulfilled. A railroad man worked in the same village, and a passionate love affair developed between them.

We know little of their story. We are cognizant only that he betrayed her. One day in November, 1909, putting a bullet through his temple, he killed himself. The young woman became disconsolate. Like Job, she cried aloud to the skies that had allowed this to happen. From that valley lost in the barren, burning mountains of Chile came a voice that men heard far and near. A banal tragedy of every day life lost its private character and became a part of world literature. It was then that Lucila Godoy y Alcayaga became Gabriela Mistral. The provincial little school teacher, this young colleague of Miss Lagerlöf of Marbacka, was to become the spiritual queen of all Latin America.

As these poems written as a memorial to death became connected with the name of a new poet, the somber and passionate verses of Gabriela Mistral began to spread throughout all South America. However, it was not until 1922 that she published in New York her greatest collection of poems, *Desolacion, Despair*. These are the tears of a mother that fall upon a book and, in the fifteenth poem, tears that flow over the son of death, a son that never was born.

> A son, a son, a son! I wanted a son of yours
> and mine, in those distant days of burning bliss
> when my bones would tremble at your least murmur
> and my brow would glow with a radiant mist.

I said *a son*, as a tree in spring
lifts its branches yearning toward the skies,
a son with innocent mien and anxious mouth,
and wondering, wide and Christ-like eyes.

His arms like a garland entwine around my neck,
the fertile river of my life is within him pent,
and from the depths of my being over all the hills
a sweet perfume spreads its gentle scent.

We look as we pass at a mother big with child,
whose lips are trembling and whose eyes are a prayer.
When deep in love we walk through the crowd,
the wonder of a babe's sweet eyes makes us stare......

Gabriela Mistral shared her maternal love with the children whom she taught. It was for them that she wrote those simple songs and those rounds collected in Madrid in 1924 under the title, *Tenura, Tenderness*. Once in her honor four thousand Mexican children sang her rounds. Gabriela Mistral became the poet of motherhood by adoption.

It was not until 1938 in Buenos Aires that, for the benefit of the young victims of the Spanish Civil War, her third great collection, *Tala*, appeared—a title which might be translated as *Devastation* but which also means a children's game. In contrast with the pathetic mood of *Desolacion*, *Tala* exhales the cosmic calm that envelops the South American earth whose perfume reaches unto us. We find ourselves anew in the garden, hear anew her intimate conversations with nature and with things. Through a curious mixture of holy hymns and naïve songs for children, of poems about bread and wine, salt, wheat, water—this water that one might very well bend to the needs of thirsty men—sing the primitive needs of human life.

From her maternal hand this poet offers us her potion, which has the savor of earth and which quenches the thirst of the heart. It is a part of that source that flowed from the Isles of Greece for Sappho, and for Gabriela Mistral in the valley of the Elqui, the source of poetry that never dries up on the earth.

Gabriela Mistral, you have made a very long voyage in order to hear so short a speech. Within a few minutes I have related for the countrymen of Selma Lagerlöf, as if it were a story, the amazing journey that has taken you from the desk of a school mistress to the throne of poetry. It is to render homage to the riches of Spanish American literature that we address ourselves today especially to its queen, the poet of *Desolacion*, who has become the great singer of mercy and motherhood. From the hands of her Royal Majesty, I beg you to receive the Nobel Prize for Literature which the Swedish Academy awards you.

HJ. GULLBERG, PH. LITT.,
Member of the Swedish Academy

Cradle Songs

CLOSE TO ME

Tiny fleece of my own flesh
woven deep within me,
tiny fleece so hating cold,
sleep close to me!

The partridge sleeps in the clover
alert to the barking dogs:
but my breathing does not disturb you.
Sleep close to me!

Trembling little blade of grass
frightened at life,
do not turn loose my breasts:
sleep close to me!

I who have lost everything
shiver at the thought of sleep.
Do not slip from my arms:
sleep close to me!

I AM NOT LONELY

The night is left lonely
from the hills to the sea.
But I, who cradle you,
I am not lonely!

The sky is left lonely
should the moon fall in the sea.
But I, who cling to you,
I am not lonely!

The world is left lonely
and all know misery.
But I, who hug you close,
I am not lonely!

CRADLE SONG

The sea cradles
its millions of stars divine.
Listening to the seas in love,
I cradle the one who is mine.

The errant wind in the night
cradles the wheat.
Listening to the winds in love,
I cradle my sweet.

God Our Father cradles
His thousands of worlds without sound.
Feeling His hand in the darkness,
I cradle the babe I have found.

NIGHT

Because you sleep, my little one,
the sunset will no longer glow:
Now nothing brighter than the dew
nor whiter than my face you know.

Because you sleep, my little one,
nothing on the highroad do we see,
nothing sighs except the river,
nothing is except me.

The plain is turning into mist,
the sky's blue breath is still.
Like a hand upon the world
silence works its will.

Not only do I rock to sleep
my baby with my singing,
but the whole world goes to sleep
to the sway of my cradle swinging.

YOU HAVE ME

Sleep, my little one,
sleep and smile,
for the night-watch of stars
rocks you awhile.

Drink in the light,
and happy be.
All good you have
in having me.

Sleep, my little one,
sleep and smile,
for the earth in love
rocks you awhile.

Look at the bright rose,
red as can be.
Reach out to the world
as you reach out to me.

Sleep, my little one,
sleep and smile,
For God in the shade
rocks you awhile.

CHARM

This child is as charming
as the sweetest winds that blow:
if he suckles me while I'm sleeping
he drinks, and I do not know.

This child is sweeter than the river
that circles the hill with its crook.
This son of mine is more beautiful
than the world on which he steals a look.

This child has greater riches
than to heaven or earth belong—
on my breast he has ermine,
and velvet in my song.

His little body is so small
it seems a tiny seed so fine:
weighing less than dreams weigh,
no one sees him, yet he's mine.

SAD MOTHER

Sleep, sleep, master mine,
without worry, without fear,
even though my soul sleeps not,
even though I do not rest.

Sleep, sleep, and in the night
may you a lesser murmur be
than a blade of grass
or the silk of fleece.

In you let my flesh sleep,
my worry and my fear.
In you let my eyes close.
May my heart sleep in you.

GENTILITIES

When I am singing to you,
on Earth wrongdoing ceases:
all is sweetness at your temples:
the gulley and the patch of brambles.

When I am singing to you
evil is erased from all:
gentle as your eyelids
become the lion and the jackal.

BITTER SONG

Little one, let's play at
being king and queen.

This green field is yours.
To whom else could it belong?
The waving fields of grain
for you are growing strong.

This whole valley is yours.
To whom else could it belong?
So that we might enjoy them,
orchards give us honey.

(No, it's not true that you shiver
like the Child of Bethlehem,
and that the breasts of your mother
are going dry through wrong!)

The sheep is growing wooly
with the fleece I'll weave so strong.
And the flocks all are yours.
To whom else could they belong?

The milk flowing sweet from udders
in stables at evensong,
and the gathering of the harvests
to whom else could they belong?

(No, it's not true that you shiver
like the Child of Bethlehem,
and that the breasts of your mother
are going dry through wrong!)

Yes, little one, let's play
at being king and queen.

FEAR

I do not want them to turn
my child into a swallow;
she might fly away into the sky
and never come down again to my doormat;
or nest in the eaves where my hands
could not comb her hair.
I do not want them to turn
my child into a swallow.

I do not want them to make
my child into a princess.
In tiny golden slippers how could
she play in the field?
And when night came, no longer
would she lie by my side.
I do not want them to make
my child into a princess.

And I would like even less
that one day they crown her queen.
They would raise her to a throne
where my feet could not climb.
I could not rock her to sleep
when nighttime came.
I do not want them to make
my child into a queen.

LITTLE LAMB

Little lamb of mine
with such softness blest,
your grotto of velvet moss
is my breast.

Flesh as white
as a moonray is white,
all else I forget
to be your cradle tonight.

I forget about the world
and want only to make
greater my breasts
for your hunger's sake.

For your fiesta, son of mine,
other fiestas end—
I only know that you
on me depend.

DEW

This was a rose
kissed by the dew:
this was my breast
my son knew.

Little leaves meet,
soft not to harm him,
and the wind makes a detour
not to alarm him.

He came down one night
from the great sky;
for him she holds her breath
so he won't cry.

Happily quiet,
not a sound ever:
rose among roses
more marvellous never.

This was a rose
kissed by the dew:
this was my breast
my son knew.

DISCOVERY

I found this child
when I went to the country:
asleep I discovered him
among the sprigs of grain . . .

Or maybe it was while
cutting through the vineyard:
searching in its branches
I struck his cheek . . .

Because of this, I fear
when I am asleep,
he might melt as frost does
on the grapevines . . .

MY SONG

The song that I have sung
for sad children,
out of pity
sing to me.

The song that I have crooned
suffering children,
now that I am hurt,
sing to me.

The cruel light stabs my eyes
and any sound upsets me.
The song to which I rocked him,
sing to me.

When I was knitting them
soft as the softness of ermine,
I did not know that my poor soul
was like a child.

The song that I have sung
for sad children,
out of pity
sing to me.

Poems for Mothers

POET'S NOTE

One afternoon, walking through a poor street in Temuco, I saw a quite ordinary woman sitting in the doorway of her hut. She was approaching childbirth, and her face was heavy with pain. A man came by and flung at her an ugly phrase that made her blush. At that moment I felt toward her all the solidarity of our sex, the infinite pity of one woman for another, and I passed on thinking, "One of us must proclaim (since men have not done so) the sacredness of this painful yet divine condition. If the mission of art is to beautify all in an immensity of pity, why have we not, in the eyes of the impure, purified this?" So I wrote these poems with an almost religious meaning.

Some women who, because of high social standing, feel it necessary to close their eyes to cruel but inevitable realities, have made of these poems a vile commentary—which saddened me for their sakes. They even went so far as to insinuate that they should be dropped from my book. . . . . No! Here they remain, dedicated to those women capable of seeing that the sacredness of life begins with maternity which is, in itself, holy. They will understand the deep tenderness with which this woman who cares for the children of others, looks upon the mothers of all the children in the world.

GABRIELA MISTRAL

HE KISSED ME

He kissed me and now I am someone else; someone
else in the pulse that repeats the pulse of my
own veins and in the breath that mingles with my
breath. Now my belly is as noble as my heart.

And even on my breath is found the breath of
flowers; all because of the one who rests gently
in my being, like dew on the grass!

WHAT WILL IT BE LIKE?

What will it be like? For a long time I looked at
the petals of a rose. I touched them with delight;
I would like their softness for his cheeks. And I
played in a tangle of brambles, because I would like his
hair dark and tangled that way. But if it is brownish,
with the rich color of the red clays that potters love,
I won't care, either, or if his stringy hair is as plain
as was my life.

I watch the hollows in the mountains when they are filling
with mist, and from the mist I make the shape of a little
girl, a very sweet little girl: that mine could well be.

But, more than anything else, I want its look to have the
sweetness that he has in his look, and may the light timbre
of its voice be like his when he speaks to me, for in the
one that is coming, I want to love the one who kissed me.

WISDOM

Now I know why I have had twenty summers of sunshine on my
head and it was given me to gather flowers in the fields.
Why, I once asked myself on the most beautiful of days,
this wonderful gift of warm sun and cool grass?

Like the blue cluster, I took in light for the sweetness
I am to give forth. That which is deep within me comes
into being, drop by drop, from the wine of my veins.

For this I prayed, to receive in the name of God the
clay with which he would be made. And when with trembling
pulse I read a poem for him, its beauty burns me like a
live coal so that he catches from my own flesh fire
that can never be extinguished.

SWEETNESS

Because of the sleeping child I carry, my footsteps
have grown silent. And my whole heart is reverent since
it bears the mystery.

My voice is soft like a mute of love, for I am afraid
to awaken it.

With my eyes in passing faces now, I seek this pain of
mine in other entrails, hoping that seeing me, others
understand why my cheek is pale.

I stir the grasses where quail nestle, tenderly afraid.
And through the countryside I go quietly, cautiously:
I believe that trees and things have sleeping children
over whom they hover watching.

SISTER

Today I saw a woman plowing a furrow. Her hips are broad, like mine, for love, and she goes about her work bent over the earth.

I caressed her waist; I brought her home with me. She will drink rich milk from my own glass and bask in the shade of my arbors growing pregnant with the pregnancy of love. And if my own breasts be not generous, my son will put his lips to hers, that are rich.

PRAYER

Oh, no! How could God let the bud of my breasts go dry when
He himself so swelled my girth? I feel my breasts growing,
rising like water in a wide pool, noiselessly. And their
great sponginess casts a shadow like a promise across my belly.

Who in all the valley could be poorer than I if my breasts
never grew moist?

Like those jars that women put out to catch the dew of night,
I place my breasts before God. I give Him a new name, I call
Him the Filler, and I beg of him the abundant liquid of life.
Thirstily looking for it, will come my son.

SENSITIVE

I no longer play in the meadows and I am afraid now to
swing back and forth with the girls. I am like a branch
full of fruit.

I am weak, so weak that the scent of roses made me faint
at siesta time when I went down into the garden. And the
simple singing of the wind or that drop of blood in the
sky when the afternoon gives its last gasp, troubles me,
floods me with sadness. Just from the look of my master,
if it is a harsh look tonight, I could die.

If he suffers within me I grow pale; grief overtakes me
at his hidden pressure, and I could die from a single
motion of this one I can not see.

But do not think that only while I carry him, will he be
entangled within me. When he shall roam free on the
highways, even though he is far away from me, the wind that
lashes him will tear at my flesh, and his cry will be in my
throat, too. My grief and my smile begin in your face, my
son.

FOR HIM

For his sake, for him now lulled to sleep like a
thread of water in the grass, do not hurt me, do not
give me work to do. Forgive me everything: my irritation
at the way the table is set and my hatred of noise.

You may tell me about the problems of the house,
its worries and its tasks, after I have tucked him away
in his covers.

On my forehead, on my breast, wherever you touch me,
he is, and he would moan if you hurt me.

QUIETNESS

Now I cannot go into the streets: I sense the blush of my
great girdle and the deep dark circles under my eyes. But
bring to me here, put right here beside me a pot full of
flowers, and slowly play soft strings: for his sake I want
to be flooded with beauty.

I put roses on my body, and over him who sleeps I say ageless
verses. In the arbor hour after hour I gather the acid of
the sun. I want to distill within me honey as the fruit does.
I feel in my face the wind from the pine groves.

Let the light and the winds color and cleanse my blood.
To rinse it, I will no longer hate, no longer gossip—only
love!

Because in this stillness, in this quietude, I am knitting
a body, a miraculous body with veins, and face, and eyes,
and heart quite clean.

LITTLE WHITE GARMENTS

I knit tiny socks of wool, cut soft diapers: I want to make
everything with my own hands. He will come out of my own
body, he will be a part of my own perfume.

Soft fleece of a sheep: this summer they shear it for him.
For eight months its wool grew sponge-like and the January
moon bleached it. Now there are no little needles of thistle
or thorns of bramble in it. Equally soft is the fleece of my
flesh where he has slept.

Such little white garments! He looks at them through my eyes
and he laughs, guessing how very, very soft they will be . . .

IMAGE OF THE EARTH

I had never before seen the true image of the Earth. The Earth looks like a woman with a child in her arms (with her creatures in her wide arms).

Now I know the maternal feeling of things. The mountain that looks down at me is a mother, too, and in the afternoons the mist plays like a child around her shoulders and about her knees.

Now I remember a cleft in the valley. In its deep bed a stream went singing, hidden by a tangle of crags and brambles. I am like that cleft; I feel singing deep within me this little brook, and I have given it my flesh for a cover of crags and brambles until it comes up toward the light.

TO MY HUSBAND

Husband, do not embrace me. You caused it to rise from the
depths of me like a water lily. Let me be like still water.

Love me, love me now a little more! I, so small, will
duplicate you on all the highways. I, so poor, will give
you other eyes, other lips, through which you may enjoy the
world; I, so frail, will split myself asunder for love's
sake like a broken jar, that the wine of life might flow.

Forgive me! I walk so clumsily, so clumsily serve your
glass; but you filled me like this and gave me this strangeness
with which I move among things.

Treat me more than ever kindly. Do not roughly stir my
blood; do not disturb my breathing.

Now I am nothing but a veil; all my body is a veil beneath
which a child sleeps.

MOTHER

My mother came to see me; she sat right here beside me,
and, for the first time in our lives, we were two sisters
who talked about a great event to come.

She felt the trembling of my belly and she gently uncovered
my bosom. At the touch of her hands to me it seemed as if
all within me half-opened softly like leaves, and up into
my breasts shot the spurt of milk.

Blushing, full of confusion, I talked with her about my
worries and the fear in my body. I fell on her breasts,
and all over again I became a little girl sobbing in her
arms at the terror of life.

TELL ME, MOTHER

Mother, tell me all you have learned from your own
pain. Tell me how he is born and how from within me
all entangled comes a little body.

Tell me if he will seek my breast alone, or if I
should offer it to him, coaxing.

Now teach me the science of love, mother. Show me
new caresses, gentle ones, gentler than those of a
husband.

How, in days to come, shall I wash his little head?
And how shall I swaddle him so as not to hurt him?

Teach me that lullaby, mother, you sang to rock me
to sleep. It will make him sleep better than any
other songs.

DAWN

All night I suffered, all night my body trembled
to deliver its offering. There is the sweat of
death on my temples; but it is not death, it is
life!

And I call you now Infinite Sweetness, God, that
you release it gently.

Let it be born! And let my cry of pain rise in
the dawn, braided into the singing of birds!

HOLY LAW

They say that life has flown from my body, that my
veins have spouted like wine presses: but I feel only
the relief a breast knows after a long sigh.

"Who am I," I say to myself, "to have a son on my knee?"
And I myself answer, "A woman who loved, and whose love,
when he kissed me, asked for eternity."

Let the Earth observe me with my son in my arms, and
bless me, because now I am fruitful like the palm trees
and furrows in the earth.

For the Saddest of Mothers

THROWN OUT

My father said he would get rid of me, yelled at my mother
that he would throw me out this very night.

The night is mild; by the light of the stars, I might find
my way to the nearest village; but suppose he is born at such
a time as this? My sobs perhaps have aroused him; perhaps he
wants to come out now to see my face covered with tears.
But he might shiver in the naked air, although I would cover him.

WHY DID YOU COME?

Why did you come? Nobody will love you although you are
beautiful, son of mine. Though you smile so cutely
like the other children, like the smallest of my little
brothers, nobody will kiss you but me, son of mine. And
though your little hands flutter about looking for toys, you will
have for your toys only my breasts and the beads of my
tears, son of mine.

Why did you come, since the one who created you hated you
when he felt you in my belly?

But no! For me you came; for me who was alone, alone until he
held me in his arms, son of mine!

Grain Divine

PRAYER

Lord, you know with what frenzy fine
Your help for strangers I have often sought.
Now I come to plead for one who was mine,
honeycomb of my mouth, spring of my drought.

Lime of my bones, sweet reason to be,
birdsong at my ear, a belt my waist to trim.
I have sought help for others who meant nothing to me.
Do not turn Your head now when I plead for him.

I tell You he was good, and I say
his heart like a flower in his breast did sing,
gentle of nature, frank as the light of day,
bursting with miracles as is the Spring.

Unworthy of my pleas is he, You sternly say,
since no sign of prayer crossed his fevered face
and one day, with no nod from You, he went away,
shattering his temples like a fragile vase.

But I tell you, Lord, I once caressed
his gentle and tormented heart—
as a lily might his brow have pressed—
and found it silky as a bud when petals part.

You say he was cruel? You forget I loved him ever.
He knew my wounded flesh was his to shatter.
Now the waters of my gladness he disturbs forever?
I loved him! You know, I loved him—so that does not matter.

To love (as You well understand) is a bitter task—
eyelids wet with tears may be,
kisses in prickly tresses may bask,
beneath them guarding eyes of ecstasy.

To welcome the chill of iron one may choose
when loving flesh its thrust encloses.
And the Cross (You recall, Oh, King of the Jews)
may be gently borne like a sheaf of roses.

So here I am, Lord, my head in the dust,
pleading with You through a dusk unending,
through all the dusks that bear I must
if You should prove unbending.

I shall wear down your ears with prayers and with cries,
licking the hem of your garment like a dog full of fears—
never to avoid me anymore Your eyes,
or your feet escape the hot rain of my tears.

Grant him forgiveness at last! Then all winds will blow
rich with a hundred vials of perfume,
all waters will sparkle, all cobblestones glow,
and the wilderness burst into bloom.

From the eyes of wild beasts gentle tears will flow,
and the mountains You forged of stone will understand
and weep through their white eyelids of snow:
the whole earth will learn of forgiveness at Your hand.

POEM OF THE SON

I

A son, a son, a son! I wanted a son of yours
and mine, in those distant days of burning bliss
when my bones would tremble at your least murmur
and my brow would glow with a radiant mist.

I said *a son*, as a tree in spring
lifts its branches yearning toward the skies,
a son with innocent mien and anxious mouth,
and wondering, wide and Christ-like eyes.

His arms like a garland entwine around my neck,
the fertile river of my life is within him pent,
and from the depths of my being over all the hills
a sweet perfume spreads its gentle scent.

We look as we pass at a mother big with child,
whose lips are trembling and whose eyes are a prayer.
When deep in love we walk through the crowd,
the wonder of a babe's sweet eyes makes us stare.

Through sleepless nights full of joy and dreams
no fiery lust invaded my bed.
For him who would be born swaddled in song,
I hollowed my breasts to pillow his head.

The sun never seemed too warm to bathe him;
but my lap I hated as too rough a place.
My heart beat wildly at so wonderful a gift,
and tears of humility streamed down my face.

Of death's vile destruction I had no fear,
for the child's eyes would free your eyes from such doom,
and I would not mind walking beneath death's dark stare
in the brilliance of morning or at evening's gloom.

61

Now I am thirty years old, and my brow is streaked
with the precocious ashes of death./And slow tears
like eternal rain at the poles,/
salty, bitter, and cold, water my years./

While the pine burns with a gentle flame,/
musing, I think it would have been meet
that my son be born with my own weary mouth,
my bitter heart and my voice of defeat.

With your heart like a poisonous fruit,/
and me whom your lips would again betray,/
for forty moons he might not have slept on my breast;
and because he was yours, he might have gone away.

In what flowering orchards, beside what running waters
in what springtime might he have cleansed his blood of my sorrow,
though I wandered afar in gentler climes,
while it coursed through his veins in some mystical tomorrow?

The fear that some day from his mouth hot with hate
he might say to me, as I to my father did protest,
"Why was your weeping flesh so fertile
as to fill with nectar a mother's breast?"

I find bitter joy in that you sleep now
deep in a bed of earth, and I cradle no child,
for I sleep, too, with no cares, no remorse,
beneath my tangle of brambles wild.

Since I may no longer close my eyes
like a crazy woman I hear voices from outer space,
and with twisted mouth on torn knees I would kneel
if I saw him pass with my pain in his face.

To me God's respite never would be given:
through his innocent flesh the wicked wound me now:
for through all eternity my blood will cry aloud
in my son ecstatic of eye and brow.

Blessed be my breast in which kin is lost
and blessed be my belly in which they die!
The face of my mother will no longer cross the world
nor her voice in the wind change to sorrow's cry.

Forests decayed to ashes will rise a hundred times
to fall again a hundred times by axe or nature's blight.
But in the month of harvest I will fall to rise no more:
me and mine shall disappear in endless night.

As though I were paying the debt of a whole race,
like cells in a beehive, my breast fills with pain.
Each passing hour to me seems a lifetime,
a bitter river flowing seaward is each vein.

I am blind to the sun and blind to the wind
for which my poor dead ones so anxiously long.
And my lips are weary of fervent prayers that,
before I grow mute, my mouth pours into song.

I did not plant for my own granary, nor teach in hope
of loving arms' support when death I might meet
and my broken body sustain me no longer,
and my hand grope for the winding sheet.

I taught the children of others, trusting only in You
to fill my granary with grain divine.
Our Father Who art in heaven, lift up this beggar.
Should I die tonight, let me be Thine.

Many years from now, when I am a little mound of silent dust, play with me, with the earth of my heart and my bones. Should a mason gather me up, he would make me into a brick, and I would be stuck forever in a wall, and I hate quiet corners. If they put me into the wall of a prison, I would blush with shame at hearing a man sob. Or if I became the wall of a school, I would suffer from not being able to sing with you in the mornings.

I had rather be dust that you play with on the country roads. Pound me, because I have been yours. Scatter me, as I did you. Stomp me because I never gave you truth entire and beauty whole. O, I mean, sing and run above me that I might kiss your precious foot prints.

Say a pretty verse when you have me in your hands, and I will run with pleasure through your fingers. Uplifted at the sight of you, in your eyes I will look for the curly heads of those I taught.

And when you have made of me some sort of statue, shatter it each time, as each time before children shattered me in tenderness and sorrow.

CHILDREN'S HAIR

Soft hair, hair that has all the softness in the world, how could I be happy dressed in silk, if I did not have you in my lap? Each passing day is sweet and nourishing only because of those hours when it runs through my hands.

Put it close to my cheek; rest it in my lap like flowers; braid it into me to ease my sorrows; strengthen the dying light with it.

When I am in heaven, may God give me no angel's wings to soothe the hurt in my heart; spread instead across the sky the hair of the children I loved, and let their hair sweep forever in the wind across my face.

from *Tala, Ternura* and *Lagar*

Earth and Women

DOVES

On the rooftop of my siesta
in the drowsy afternoon,
the footsteps of doves evoke
little shells and sand.

The white siesta, the stern house,
and the sick woman crying below
do not hear the anise seed, backstitch sounds
of the footsteps of doves.

I lift my hand with its grain
like an old indulgent mother,
and my body full of doves
sings reverberating.

Three bear with me still
and their harsh tumult I hear
until they fly away in all directions
and for me only a single dove remains.

I do not know what voices call me
nor what siesta smothers me:
  Epiphany in my lap!
  Dove! . . . Dove!

HELPERS

While yet the child sleeps within me
knowing nothing of this earth,
to help me complete him
the grass makes his hair,
the date palm his tiny fingers
and white wax his fingernails.
Snails give him a way of hearing
and the red strawberry his tongue,
and the brook brings him laughter
while the mountain gives him patience.

Since some things are left unfinished,
I am confused and ashamed:
hardly has he temples, hardly speech,
hardly a shape that can be noticed.

Those who fetch things go and come,
in and out of the door
bringing little ears of dried apricots
and mother-of-pearl teeth.

Three Nativities, and there will be another,
with his ankles around his head.
He will be stocky, he will be straight
as the pines on the slope of the hill.

Then like a crazy woman I will go
crying his name through the villages
proclaiming it so all the meadows
and even the hills will hear.

EARTH AND THE WOMAN

While the world is still light
and my child is wide awake,
in his face there's nothing
but a winking, winking, winking.

The poplar grove winks
with her yellow fingers,
while behind her clouds
pirouette like baby goats.

The katydid at noonday
winks with its hindlegs,
while an impudent little breeze
winks with its shirt tail.

When night descends the cricket
winks ever so slyly,
and as the stars come out,
they wink at me with saintly winks.

I say to that other Mother,
where the two roads flood each other,
Put your Little One to sleep,
So mine will go to sleep.

And that most Indulgent One,
Radiance of the crossroads,
answers, *You put yours to sleep—*
So mine will go to sleep.

The blood red rose
I gathered yesterday,
and the fire and cinnamon
of the carnation,

Bread baked with
anise seed and honey,
and a fish in a bowl
that makes a glow:

All this is yours,
baby born of woman,
if you'll *just*
go to sleep.

A rose, I say!
I say a carnation!
Fruit, I say!
And I say honey!

A fish that glitters!
And more, I say—
if you will *only*
sleep till day.

ASLEEP

My body swaying,
Cradling my son,
I mill the whole world
with my living pulse.

The world, in the arms
of this miller woman,
begins to change
into a mist of whiteness.

The shape of the world
comes into my room,
through timber and glass,
covering mother and child.

It is all the hills
and all the rivers,
all ever created,
all ever born.

I sway, I sway,
and watch disappearing
the ever so sensitive
body they gave me.

Now I see neither
cradle nor child,
and it seems the world
has utterly vanished.

I cry out to Him who gave me
the world and my son—
and I awaken myself with
my own crying.

THE STABLE

When midnight came
and the Child's first cry arose,
a hundred beasts awakened
and the stable became alive.

And drawing near they came
reaching out toward the Child
a hundred eager necks
like a forest swaying.

An ox whose eyes were as tender
as though filled with dew,
lowered its head to breathe
quietly in His face.

Against Him rubbed a lamb
with the softest of soft fleece,
and two baby goats squatted,
licking His hands.

The walls of the stable
unnoticed were covered
with pheasants and with geese
and cocks and with blackbirds.

The pheasants flew down
and swept over the Child
tails of many colors;
while the geese with wide bills
smoothed His pallet of straw;
and a swarm of blackbirds
became a veil rising and falling
above the new born.

The Virgin, confused among such horns
and whiteness of breathing,
fluttered hither and yon
unable to pick up her Child.

And Joseph arrived laughing
to help her in her confusion,
and the upset stable was like
a forest in the wind.

INDIAN CHRISTMAS

Mother with no Christmas gifts
large or small anywhere,
dreaming at midnight,
I give my child quite bare.

High amid the harsh stubble
in the air of the Andes rare,
the only gift I have to give
is my child quite bare.

The wind from La Puna
that cries so sharply there
has no cry like the cry
of my child quite bare.

God watches over all:
by Him to do my share,
on Holy Night I offer
my child quite bare.

SEED

I

Sleep, tiny son, like seed
at the moment of sowing
in days of seeding
or in months of blindness.

Sleep, tiny pit of a cherry,
morsel of strange flavor,
warm sun-colored fruit
from the tanned cheek of Sindbad.

Sleep as an old tale does
that makes folks laugh and cry.
Such a little trifle
you are and yet are not.

II

Tiny being that mirrors
bigger things to come,
breast full of moonbeams
scattered in fields to plow.

Hands on oars
of the hardest wood there is,
arrow for the hills
where pheasants are hunted.

Sleep, heir of adventures
out of the sea,
godchild of the ancient voyages
of Columbus and Genghis Khan.

Heir of adorations
glory of men and gods,
and figure of Christ Jesus
dividing loaves and fishes.

LITTLE CHILD

Funny little night-one
joker of mine,
yes-you-are, no-you're-not
of this world, sleeping child.

Little breath and big
that I hear but do not see,
Clam of the night
that I call son.

Blade of pretty space,
blade of whispering breeze,
blade of a great star,
sleeping child.

Each hour you sleep,
becoming lighter, lighter.
After midnight
you are hardly a child.

Thick slab, heavy
beams, rough
linen, harsh chant
over my son.

Cruel air, scalding
stars, stubborn
river, obstinate owl
over my son.

In the great night
so small a child,
so little proof and sign,
so tiny a mark.

Shame on such a night,
on such a river
and such a mother,
sleeping child.

Shrink the earth
with your going.
Shock the globe
touching this child.

Let the night change you
into something divine,
and me into the urn of your dreams,
sleeping child.

Sleep, my very own
blood that you make double,
life of mine that sways
on a branch of blood.

Moss of my dreams
in which you jell,
sleep with your savor
of milk and blood.

Son of mine still not acquainted
with pineapples or aloes,
knowing only within me
pomegranates of blood.

Lacking blood of your own,
your pulse beats with mine.
Sleep as you do quite satisfied
with milk and with blood.

Crystal translucence and
illumination of blood;
lantern alight with my blood
that lights me.

The red wine of my blood
lifted from within me,
your banner in which my blood
rises and falls.

On his own he comes and goes
to bring back my well-being,
and plays with the sand dune
casting the shadow of my blood.

At night, if I am lost,
my blood will bring him to me.
And at night, if I lose him
I will find him through his blood.

SONG OF THE FISHERFOLK

Little daughter of fisherfolk
who has a way with wind and waves,
may you sleep covered with sea shells,
may you sleep entangled in nets.

Sleep atop the dune that lifts you high,
listening to the sea-nurse who,
ever wilder, rocks you the more.

Nets that will not let me keep you
fill my lap,
for should I break their knots
I might break your luck.

Sleep better now than you
could in your own cradle,
mouth full of sand,
dreams full of fish.

Two fish at your knees,
one with head and breast of silver
leaping and jumping,
the other aglow . . .

THOSE WHO DON'T DANCE

A crippled child once said,
"How can I dance?"
We told her that she should
start her heart to dancing.

Then said the deformed one,
"How can I ever sing?"
We told her that she should
start her heart to singing.

Said the poor dead cocklebur,
"How ever can I dance?"
We told it, "Let the wind
set your heart to flying."

God asked from above,
"How can I leave the sky?"
We told Him to come down
and dance with us in the brightness.

All in the valley are dancing
Together beneath the sun.
May the heart of whoever is missing
Turn to dust and ashes.

GIVEN BACK

Over the face of my son
who sleeps, let sands
of the dunes descend,
and cane flowers,
and the foam that flies
from the waterfall . . .

Yet it is only sleep
that descends, sleep
that falls on his mouth,
sleep across his shoulder,
to steal from me his body
along with his soul.

Thus they go covering him
with so much manna
that by night I have
no son at all,
mother blind with shadows,
mother robbed.

Only when the blessed sun
bathes him at last
is my beautiful fruit
returned to me all clean
and put intact
upon my lap.

MAIMED

Since a clam caught my little finger,
and since the clam fell into the sand,
and since the sea swallowed up the sand,
and since a whaler fished it up from the sea
and since the whaler went to Gibraltar;
and since in Gibraltar fishermen sing:
"Something new we bring up from the sea,
something new, a girl's little finger—
let the one who lost it come for it,"

Let them give me a boat to go get it,
and give me a captain for the boat,
and give me wages for the captain,
and for wages let him demand the city:
Marseilles with towers and plazas and boats,
the very best city in all the world—
which would not be beautiful with a little girl
whose little finger the sea has stolen—
as the whalers proclaim it far and wide
watching and waiting at Gibraltar.

THE PARROT

The green and yellow parrot,
the saffron and green parrot,
called me "ugly," squawking
with his devilish bill.

I am not ugly, for if I am ugly,
then my mother who looks like the sun is ugly,
the light that is part of my mother is ugly,
and the wind is ugly that sounds in her voice,
and ugly is the water that reflects her body,
and ugly is the world and He who created it . . .

The green and yellow parrot,
green and shimmering parrot,
calls me "ugly" because he has not eaten,
so I take him bread and wine,
for I am getting tired of looking at him
up there always posed, always shimmering.

THE RAT

A rat ran after a deer
and the deer after a jaguar,
and the jaguars after the buffalos,
and the buffalos after the sea . . .

Catch, catch them as they go!
Catch the rat, catch the deer,
catch the buffalos, and on to the sea.

Look at the rat in front
carrying wool in his paws for trimming,
and with the wool he trims my dress
and with the dress I am going to get married.

Up and over the plain they go,
breathlessly on, ahead without stopping,
flying toward the bride, and toward the procession,
toward the carriage and the wedding veil.

THE PEACOCK

The wind blew and took away the clouds
and with the clouds went a peacock.
The peacock was meant for my hand
but my hand will remain barren—
the same hand I gave this morning
to the king who took me to wife.
Oh, for the sky! Oh, for the wind, and the clouds
that departing took with them the peacock!

LARKS

They came down in a patch of wheat,
and, as we drew near,
the flock flew away
and left the startled field quite empty.

In the thicket they look like fire;
when they rise, like silver darting.
And they go by even before they go,
cutting through your wonder.

Our poor eyes, knowing only
that the whole flock has gone,
cry "Larks!" to those who rise,
and are lost, and sing.

In the sorely wounded air
they leave us full of yearning,
with a wonder and a quiver
in body and in soul . . .

Larks, son! Above us sweep
the larks across the plain!

LITTLE WORKMAN

Mother, when I am big,
Oh, what a boy you'll have!
I will lift you in my arms
as the warm wind lifts the grasses.

I will rest you on a heap of unthreshed grain,
or carry you to the sea,
or lift you up on a hill top,
or drop you on your threshold.

And what a house I will build you,
your little boy become a giant,
and what loving shade
its eaves will give you.

And I will give you an orchard
and your apron will tire of holding
all its fruit, its thousands,
and more thousands of fruit.

Or better still, I'll make you tapestries
from the braided rushes,
or even better, give you a mill
that chatters while you make bread.

Oh, count, just count the windows
and the doors of your house!
Count, just count the wonders
if you can!

Richness

RICHNESS

I have a true happiness
and a happiness betrayed,
the one like a rose,
the other like a thorn.
To that taken from me
I was not betrothed:
I have a true happiness
and a happiness betrayed.
And I am rich in purple
and rich in melancholy.
How well loved the rose!
And what a lover the thorn!
Like a double image
of fruits that are twins,
I have a true happiness
and a happiness betrayed.

THE CUP

I carried a cup
from one island to the other
without wasting water.
Were I to spill it, thirst would betray me;
just a drop, and the gift would be gone;
if all were lost, its owner would cry.

No cities did I greet,
nor praise their flight of towers,
nor open my arms to the great Pyramid,
nor found a family with a chorus of children.
But when I brought the cup I said,
with the morning sun in my throat,
"My arms are as free as clouds with no owner
and by invitation of the valley
my neck sways on the hill."

My hallelujah was a lie: Look at me.
My eyes are downcast toward my palms;
slowly I walk with not a diamond of water:
silently I come with no treasure,
while in my breast and through my veins
pounds my blood in anguish and in fear.

PARADISE

An engraving of gold on the wall,
and in it etched all golden
two bodies like a skein of gold.

A brilliant body that hears
and a glorious body that speaks
in the meadow where nothing speaks.

A breath that vanishes in a breath
and a face that trembles because of it
in a meadow where nothing trembles.

Remember the sad time
when both had Time
and because of it live in sorrow.

In the moment of golden anguish
when Time stopped at the threshold
like a stray dog . . .

GIVE ME YOUR HAND

Give me your hand, let's dance, we two,
give me your hand as before.
Be a single flower, me and you,
a single flower, and nothing more.

We will sing the selfsame way,
the same dance steps explore.
Like a sprig of grain we'll sway,
a single sprig, and nothing more.

Your name is Rose, Hope am I,
but in a name let's take no store,
for we will be on a hilltop high
just a dance, and nothing more.

MIDNIGHT

Delicate the midnight.
I hear the knots of the rosebush:
sap pushing upward rising to the rose.

I hear
the burning rays
of the Bengal tiger:
they do not let him sleep.

I hear
the couplet of fat
as it grows in the night
like a dune.

I hear
my mother sleeping
with two breaths.
(At the age of five
I sleep within her.)

I hear Roldan
descend and carry me
like a father,
blind with blind foam.

Then I hear nothing
except that I am falling
on the walls of Arles
bathed in sunshine . . .

WHEN SNOW FALLS

Divinely down the snow comes
    on the valley to pay a call.
Nicer than stars, the snow comes down.
    Look at it fall!

Softly it comes, comes to our doors,
    calling without a call.
So comes the Virgin, and so come dreams.
    Look at it fall!

    It stirs up the great nest
    of the sky and makes it fly.
    Feathers fall on the valley,
    feathers fall on the plain,
    and on the olive groves they lie.

Perhaps it scatters in falling, falling,
the Word of God, our Father above.
    Perhaps it's His mantle,
    perhaps His image,
    perhaps His love.

THE ROSE

The treasure at the heart of the rose
is your heart's own treasure.
Scatter it as the rose does:
your pain becomes hers to measure.

Scatter it in a song,
or in one great love's desire.
Do not resist the rose
lest you burn in its fire.

Why this sudden attack,
I don't know:
But I want to sing:
my land is not the land
of the palm tree,

Nor does my mother
come back home,
nor do I come back to her
crying in a boat.

The wish to sing I share
with three tempests
without being able to sing
in the turbulence;

For the recurring wind
in which I walk bartered,
for the hills I traverse
among the lazy chestnuts,

And a sound that sings of waters
where I don't know,
come to my breast
and are part of the cascade.

Let it fall where it falls
and yesterday did not fall,
very near my body
headlong it tumbles and calls.

I stop and listen
without going to find it:
water, my mother,
and my daughter, water!

I want to see her and can't
because I am too anxious,
ovation of water
that keeps on falling.

WOODCUTTER

The tired woodcutter
lay on the grass,
asleep in the scent
of the pine he has cut.
Where his feet went
the grasses are crushed.
His back of gold sings
and his hands are dreaming.
I see his threshold of stone,
his wife and his acres.
The things that he loves
walk by his side;
the things he has not
make him more noble,
and the sleepyhead sleeps
with no name, like a tree.

High noon stings
as if it were a javelin.
By a cool branch
his face is protected.
From him to me comes
his day like a song,
and I give him my day
like a pine newly felled.
Coming back at night
across the blind plain,
I hear women calling
the man who is late;
and he falls on my shoulders
and I have in four arrows
the name of him I kept hidden
with my blood and my breath.

CATALAN WOMEN

"The old sea of nuptial songs
will call them over and over virgins.
Maybe all of them are one
whom they call Nausicaa."

"Certainly we kiss better on the dunes
than on the thresholds of houses,
testing lips and giving lips
like almonds sweet and bitter."

"Pruners of olive groves
and grinders of almond paste,
we descend from Montserrat
to hug the head of the sea . . ."

Country with No Name

Country that is missing,
strange country,
lighter than angel
and nebulous password,
color of dead algae,
color of mist,
ageless as time
lacking ageless bliss.

No pomegranates spring
or jasmines blow,
it has neither skies
nor seas of indigo.
Your name is a name
never heard called have I,
and in country with no name
I am going to die.

Neither bridge nor boat
brought me hither.
Nobody told me
it was island or shore.
I did not seek
or discover it either.

It seems like a fable now
that I've learned it,
dreaming to stay
and dreaming to fly.
But it is my country
where I live and I die.

I was born of things
that are no country:
of lands upon lands

I had and I lost;
of children I have watched die;
and things mine no longer
to which once I said *my*.

I lost mountain ranges
where once I slept;
orchards of gold I lost
sweet with life;
islands I lost
of cane and indigo,
and I watched their shadows
close in on me
and crowds and lovers
become country.

Manes of mist
with no napes and no backs
I watched the sleeping
winds make fly
and through errant years
turn into a country,
and in country with no name
I am going to die.

STRANGER

"She speaks in a slight accent about her wild seas
with God knows what seaweeds and God knows what sands;
so old it's as if she herself were dying,
she prays to a god with no volume and no weight.
She has sown cactus and claw-like grasses
in gardens of ours that she makes strange.
She draws her breath from the panting of the desert
and loves with a passion all that it whitens,
all that never says anything and if it should
it would be like the map of another planet.
Were she to live in our midst for eighty years
it would be always as though she had just come,
speaking in a language that pants and moans
and that is understood only by beasts.
And some night when her suffering is greatest
from a death both silent and strange,
she is going to die right here among us
with nothing but her fate for a pillow."

THINGS

1.

I love the things I never had
along with those I have no more.

I touch still water
standing in chilly pastures
where not a single wind shivers
in the orchard that was my orchard.

I stare at it as it stared;
it starts me thinking strangely,
and I play with this water listlessly
as with fish or with mystery.

2.

I think of a threshold where I left
gay steps no longer with me,
and on the threshold I see a wound
covered with moss and silence.

3.

I search for a rhyme they said to me
when I was seven but now have lost.
She was a woman baking bread
and I look at her saintly mouth.

4.

An aroma ripped to threads arises;
I am very lucky if I sense it;
so thin that it has no aroma,
being but trace of almond trees.

My senses turn into a child;
I search for a name but can not guess it.
I smell the wind and all its spaces
seeking almond trees I do not find . . .

5.

Ever near a river dreams.
Forty years now that I feel it,
a humming in my blood or rather
a rhythm that they gave me.

O, River Elqui of my childhood
in which I wade upstream,
never shall I lose you; side by side
like two children, we have each other.

6.

As the Cordillera dreams,
I walk through gorges,
and keep hearing with no relief
a hissing that is almost curse.

7.

I see at the edge of the Pacific
my livid archipelago,
and left over for me from an island
is the sour scent of passion dead.

8.

A back, a back solemn and sweet,
ends the dream I dream.
It is the terminus of my road,
and when I reach it, I rest.

This indistinct and ashen back
is a dead tree trunk or is my father.
I ask no questions, nor disturb it.
Together, I keep still and sleep.

9.

I love the stone that I draw to me
from Oaxaca or Guatemala,
flushed and firm as is my face
and from whose fissure comes a breathing.

When I go to sleep, it is naked.
Why I turn it over, I do not know.
Perhaps I never had it
and what I see is my tomb.

ABSENCE

My body leaves you drop by drop,
my face leaves in a silence of the oil of death;
my hands leave in live mercury;
my feet leave in two puffs of dust.

All leaves you, all leaves us!

My voice leaves that you make a bell,
silent when we are not ourselves.
Expression leaves, dizzily entangled
in knots and bows before your eyes.
And the glance that I gave you leaves
as I look at you, juniper and elm.

I go from you with your own breath:
as the vapor from your body evaporates.
I go from you in sleeplessness and in sleep,
and from your remembrance I am erased.
And in your memory I become like those
born neither in plains nor in thickets.

I will be blood, and you will find me in the palms
of your hands and the wine of your mouth.
Your entrails I become, and I will be burned
in your footsteps I hear no more
and in your pain that pounds in the night
like the madness of seas that are lonely.

All leaves us, all leaves us!

TWO ANGELS

I have not only one angel
with flapping wings:
the angel that gives joy
and the one who gives pain
rock me like the sea
rocked by two shores,
the one of fluttering wings
and the one whose wings are still.

I know at dawn
which one will rule my day,
the one the color of flame
or the one the color of ashes,
and I give myself to them contrite
like seaweed to the wave.

Only once did they fly
all with wings together:
on the day of love
and on Epiphany.

Then they joined
their warring wings as one
and tied the knot
of life and death.

I found her standing in my path
half way across the meadow,
mistress of all who passed her way
or spoke or looked upon her.

She said to me, "Go up the mountain—
I never leave the meadow—
and gather me flowers white as snow,
sturdy and tender."

I went up the bitter mountain
seeking flowers where they whiten
half asleep and half awake
among the crags.

When I came down with my burden,
in the middle of the meadow I found her,
and frantically covered her
with a shower of white lilies.

But without looking at the whiteness
she said to me, "This time bring back
only flowers that are red.
I cannot go beyond the meadow."

I scaled the rocks with deer
and sought the flowers of madness,
those that grew so red they seemed
to live and die of redness.

When I descended happily trembling,
I gave them as my offering,
and she became as water
that from a wounded deer turns bloody.

But, like a sleepwalker, looking at me,
she said, "Go up and bring back now
golden ones, the golden ones.
I never leave the meadow."

Up the mountain straight I climbed
to search for the thickest flowers,
those the color of sun and saffron,
just born but yet eternal.

When I found her as usual
in the middle of the meadow,
I covered her once more with flowers
and left her as in a garden.

Still, crazy with gold,
she said, "Slave of mine, climb up
and gather flowers without color,
neither saffron nor of crimson—

"Those that I love in memory
of Leonara and Ligeia,
the color of sleep and the color of dreams.
I am the Mother of the Meadow."

Climbing I went up the mountain
dark now as Medea,
like a vague but certain grotto
with no tiles high gleaming.

There grew no flowers on any branches,
none bloomed among the crags,
so from the air I gathered blossoms,
cutting them lightly.

I picked them as if I were
a picker who was blind,
cutting here and there from air
and taking air as garden.

When I descended from the mountain
and went looking for the queen,
no longer pale or wild-eyed
she was strolling now:

Like a sleepwalker,
she started from the meadow,
and I followed, followed, followed
through the pasture, through the grove.

Quite loaded down with flowers,
shoulders and hands aerial,
she went on plucking them from air
and the wind became her harvest.

On she goes now with no face,
on she goes and leaves no footprints,
bearing flowers without color,
neither white nor crimson.

Still I follow, follow after
through the branches of the mist,
until she leads me to the brink
where Time dissolves . . .

OLD LION

"Your hair
is white now, too;
fear, rough voice,
mouth, *amen*.

Too late you sought,
too late you saw
eyes without brilliance,
temples deaf.

So much you suffered
to learn
the quiet hearth,
the rancid honey.

Much love and grief
it took to know
my lion gray-haired,
and such old feet!"

SONG

A woman is singing in the valley. The shadows falling blot her out, but her song spreads over the fields.

Her heart is broken, like the jar she dropped this afternoon among the pebbles in the brook. As she sings, the hidden wound sharpens on the thread of her song, and becomes thin and hard. Her voice in modulation dampens with blood.

In the fields the other voices die with the dying day, and a moment ago the song of the last slow-poke bird stopped. But her deathless heart, alive with grief, gathers all the silent voices into her voice, sharp now, yet very sweet.

Does she sing for a husband who looks at her silently in the dusk, or for a child whom her song caresses? Or does she sing for her own heart, more helpless than a babe at nightfall.

Night grows maternal before this song that goes to meet it; the stars, with a sweetness that is human, are beginning to come out; the sky full of stars becomes human and understands the sorrows of this world.

Her song, as pure as water filled with light, cleanses the plain and rinses the mean air of day in which men hate. From the throat of the woman who keeps on singing, day rises nobly evaporating toward the stars.